THE
MONSTER
WITHIN

Understanding and Overcoming Mental Health Challenges. Learn about the challenges and difficulties that arises with mental health issues, and overcoming them with the right strategies and techniques.

AMY BRADFORD

Amy Bradford

TABLE OF CONTENT

INTRODUCTION

Mental health is a crucial aspect of our overall well-being, yet it's often overlooked or stigmatized in society. However, it's time to change that narrative and prioritize our mental health. In this book, we will explore the power of mental health and how to unlock our mind's potential.

We will start by understanding mental health and how it impacts our daily lives. We'll delve into the science of positive thinking and explore various coping mechanisms for managing stress and anxiety. Next, we'll tackle the topic of depression and negative thoughts and learn how to overcome them. Building resilience through adversity is also an important aspect of mental health, and we'll show you how to do it.

Nutrition and exercise play a vital role in mental health, and we'll discuss the latest research in these areas. Additionally, we'll explore the benefits of mindfulness and meditation, as well as how to heal from trauma and move forward. Effective communication strategies are essential for maintaining mental health, and we'll cover that topic too.

Unfortunately, there's still a lot of stigma surrounding mental health, but we'll give you tools and techniques for navigating it. Finally, we'll wrap up the book with tips for maintaining mental wellness long-term.

By the end of this book, you'll have a comprehensive understanding of mental health and how to prioritize it in your life. You'll also have practical tools and techniques for maintaining mental wellness and unlocking your mind's potential. Let's get started!

CHAPTER ONE
Understanding Mental Health

Mental health refers to our emotional, psychological, and social well-being. It impacts how we think, feel, and behave in our daily lives. Mental health is just as important as physical health and should be a priority for everyone.

There are many different factors that can impact mental health, such as genetics, environment, and life experiences. Mental health disorders are common, affecting one in five adults in the United States alone. Some of the most common mental health disorders include anxiety, depression, bipolar disorder, and schizophrenia. Each disorder has its own set of symptoms and treatment options. It's important to note that mental health disorders are not a sign of weakness or personal failure. They are medical conditions that require treatment, just like any physical illness.

There are many signs and symptoms of poor mental health. These can include changes in mood, behavior, or personality, as well as physical symptoms like headaches or stomachaches. It's essential to pay attention to these signs and seek help if needed. Fortunately, there are many resources available for those struggling with mental health disorders. These can include therapy, medication, support groups, and self-care practices. It's important to find the right combination of resources for each individual's unique needs.

In addition to seeking help for mental health disorders, it's also important to prioritize mental wellness in everyday life. This can include practices like meditation, exercise, journaling, and spending time with loved ones.

By understanding mental health and the various factors that impact it, we can better prioritize our own mental wellness and seek help if needed. Remember, mental health is just as important as physical health and should be a priority for everyone.

Mental Health Disorders

Mental health disorders are medical conditions that affect the way people think, feel, and behave. There are many different types of mental health disorders, each with their own set of symptoms and treatment options.

Some of the most common mental health disorders include:

Anxiety Disorders: These disorders are characterized by excessive worry, fear, and nervousness. Examples include Generalized Anxiety Disorder, Panic Disorder, and Social Anxiety Disorder.

Mood Disorders: These disorders involve changes in mood, such as feelings of sadness, hopelessness, or elation. Examples include Depression, Bipolar Disorder, and Seasonal Affective Disorder.

Schizophrenia Spectrum Disorders: These disorders affect a person's ability to think, feel, and perceive reality. Symptoms can include delusions, hallucinations, and disorganized speech or behavior.

Personality Disorders: These disorders involve patterns of behavior, thoughts, and emotions that are inflexible and cause significant distress or impairment in daily life. Examples include Borderline Personality Disorder, Antisocial Personality Disorder, and Narcissistic Personality Disorder.

Eating Disorders: These disorders involve abnormal eating habits that can negatively affect a person's physical and mental health. Examples include Anorexia Nervosa, Bulimia Nervosa, and Binge Eating Disorder.

Mental health disorders can affect anyone, regardless of age, gender, or background. While some disorders may have a genetic component, others may be triggered by environmental factors or life experiences. It's important to seek help from a mental health professional if you are experiencing symptoms of a mental health disorder. Early intervention can lead to better outcomes and a higher quality of life.

CHAPTER TWO
Signs and Symptoms of Poor Mental Health

There are many different signs and symptoms of poor mental health. Some of these may be physical, while others may be emotional or behavioral. Here are some signs:

Changes in mood: Mood changes, such as feeling sad, irritable, or hopeless, can be a sign of poor mental health.

Changes in behavior: Changes in behavior, such as withdrawing from social activities or engaging in risky behaviors, can be a sign of poor mental health.

Physical symptoms: Physical symptoms like headaches, stomachaches, or fatigue can be a sign of poor mental health.

Factors That Impact Mental Health
There are many different factors that can impact a person's mental health. These can include genetic, environmental, and lifestyle factors.
Genetics: Some mental health disorders have a genetic component, meaning they run in families. For example, research has shown that Bipolar

Disorder and Schizophrenia may have a genetic component.

Environment: Environmental factors can also impact mental health. Traumatic events, such as abuse or neglect, can lead to the development of mental health disorders. Other environmental factors, such as poverty or social isolation, can also negatively impact mental health.

Lifestyle: Lifestyle factors, such as diet, exercise, and sleep, can impact mental health. For example, a diet high in processed foods and sugar has been linked to an increased risk of depression. Regular exercise has been shown to improve mood and reduce symptoms of anxiety and depression.

To promote good mental health, seek therapy or counseling, practicing stress-reduction techniques like meditation, and making lifestyle changes like eating a healthy diet and getting regular exercise.

CHAPTER THREE
The Science of Positive Thinking

Positive thinking is a powerful tool that can improve mental health and well-being. Studies have shown that positive thinking can lead to a reduction in symptoms of anxiety and depression, improved immune function, and increased resilience.
One way to cultivate positive thinking is through gratitude. Practicing gratitude involves focusing on the positive aspects of life and acknowledging the good things that have happened, even in difficult times. This can involve keeping a gratitude journal, writing letters of appreciation to loved ones, or simply taking a few minutes each day to reflect on the good things in life.

Another way to cultivate positive thinking is through reframing negative thoughts. Reframing involves taking a negative thought and looking at it from a different perspective. For example, instead of thinking, "I'm never going to be able to do this," try reframing the thought as, "This is a challenge, but I'm going to work on it and see what I can accomplish." Positive thinking does not mean ignoring or denying negative emotions. It's normal to experience a range of emotions, both positive and negative. However, practicing positive thinking can help to balance out negative emotions and improve overall mental well-being.

There are other strategies and techniques that can help to cultivate positive thinking and improve mental health. One of such technique is visualization. Visualization involves imagining a positive outcome or situation and focusing on the feelings associated with it. For example, if you're feeling anxious about an upcoming presentation at work, you might visualize yourself giving the presentation confidently and receiving positive feedback from your colleagues. This can help to reduce anxiety and improve confidence.

Another technique is practicing self-compassion. Self-compassion involves treating oneself with the same kindness, concern, and understanding that one would offer to a good friend. This can involve acknowledging and accepting one's imperfections, rather than criticizing or judging oneself. Research has shown that self-compassion can lead to improved mental health outcomes, including decreased symptoms of anxiety and depression.

Meditation and mindfulness practices can also be helpful for cultivating positive thinking. These practices involve focusing on the present moment and accepting one's thoughts and feelings without judgment. By practicing mindfulness and meditation, individuals can learn to become more aware of negative thought patterns and develop the skills to shift their focus towards positive thoughts and emotions.

In addition to these techniques, maintaining a healthy lifestyle can also contribute to positive thinking and improved mental health. Regular exercise, a balanced diet, and adequate sleep can all help to reduce stress and improve mood. Overall, positive thinking is an important aspect of mental health and well-being.

CHAPTER FOUR

Coping Mechanisms for Managing Stress and Anxiety

Stress and anxiety are common experiences that can impact mental health. Coping mechanisms can help individuals manage these feelings and prevent them from becoming overwhelming. One effective coping mechanism is deep breathing. Deep breathing involves taking slow, deep breaths, and can help to slow the heart rate and promote relaxation. Other relaxation techniques, such as progressive muscle relaxation or guided imagery, can also be helpful.

Regular exercise is another effective way to manage stress and anxiety. Exercise releases endorphins, which can improve mood and reduce feelings of anxiety. It can also help to improve sleep, which is important for overall mental health.

Practicing self-care is another important coping mechanism. This can involve activities such as taking a warm bath, spending time in nature, or engaging in a favorite hobby. It's important to prioritize self-care activities and make time for them regularly.

Time management skills can also be helpful for managing stress. Learning to prioritize tasks, set realistic goals, and manage time effectively can help to reduce feelings of overwhelm and prevent burnout. It's crucial to address any sources of stress or anxiety that may be ongoing or persistent. This may involve making changes in one's personal or professional life, such as setting boundaries, seeking a different job, or addressing relationship issues. In some cases, medication may also be helpful in managing symptoms of anxiety or stress.

Finally, seeking support from friends, family, or a mental health professional can be a helpful coping mechanism. Talking to someone about feelings of stress and anxiety can help to reduce their intensity and provide perspective. By using a combination of these coping mechanisms and techniques, you can effectively manage feelings of stress and anxiety and improve their overall mental health and well-being.

CHAPTER FIVE
Overcoming Depression and Negative Thoughts

Depression is a common mental health disorder that can be challenging to manage. However, there are many effective treatment options available.
Cognitive-behavioral therapy (CBT) is a type of therapy that has been shown to be effective in treating depression. CBT involves identifying negative thoughts and replacing them with more positive, realistic thoughts. This can help to improve mood and reduce symptoms of depression.

Medication can also be an effective treatment option for depression. Antidepressants work by balancing chemicals in the brain that impact mood. However, it's important to work with a mental health professional to determine the best medication and dosage.

In addition to therapy and medication, self-care activities can also be helpful in managing depression. This can involve activities such as exercise, healthy eating, and engaging in activities that bring joy.
It's important to seek help from a mental health professional if you are experiencing symptoms of depression. Depression is a serious condition that

can impact all areas of life, but with proper treatment, it can be effectively managed.

Another treatment option for depression is interpersonal therapy (IPT), which focuses on improving relationships and communication skills. This type of therapy can be especially helpful for individuals who experience depression due to difficulties in relationships or life transitions. While another aspect of managing depression is identifying and addressing underlying issues, such as trauma or unresolved emotions. This may involve working with a therapist to explore past experiences and learn coping skills to manage their impact on current life.

In some cases, alternative therapies such as acupuncture, yoga, or meditation may also be helpful in managing depression. These therapies can promote relaxation and improve mood, but it's important to work with a healthcare professional to determine the best course of treatment. Recovery from depression is a journey and may involve setbacks. It's important to be patient with oneself and continue to seek support from healthcare professionals and loved ones.

CHAPTER SIX
Building Resilience Through Adversity

Resilience is the ability to bounce back from difficult experiences. Building resilience can help individuals to manage stress, improve mental health, and navigate challenging situations. One way to build resilience is through positive self-talk. This involves replacing negative self-talk with positive, affirming messages. For example, instead of thinking, "I can't do this," try thinking, "I can do this, I have overcome challenges in the past."

Another way to build resilience is by cultivating social support. Having a strong support system can help individuals to cope with stress and overcome adversity. This can involve reaching out to friends or family members for support, joining a support group, or seeking help from a mental health professional.

Practicing self-care is also an important way to build resilience. This can involve activities such as exercise, healthy eating, and engaging in hobbies or activities that bring joy. It's important to prioritize self-care and make time for it regularly. Also, practicing mindfulness can help individuals to build resilience. Mindfulness involves paying attention to the present moment and accepting it without judgment. This can help to reduce stress and improve overall well-being.

Building resilience takes time and effort, but it is an important skill that can help individuals to overcome challenges and thrive in the face of adversity.

CHAPTER SEVEN

The Role of Nutrition and Exercise in Mental Health

Nutrition and exercise play important roles in mental health. A healthy diet can provide the nutrients needed to support brain function and improve mood. Regular exercise can release endorphins, which can improve mood and reduce symptoms of anxiety and depression.

A healthy diet should include a variety of fruits, vegetables, whole grains, lean proteins, and healthy fats. Avoiding processed foods, sugar, and unhealthy fats can also improve overall health and well-being.
Regular exercise can include activities such as walking, running, yoga, or weightlifting. It's important to find activities that are enjoyable and sustainable in order to make regular exercise a part of daily life.

In addition to a healthy diet and regular exercise, getting enough sleep is also important for mental health. Adults should aim for 7-9 hours of sleep each night in order to support overall health and well-being. It's important to remember that nutrition and exercise should be used in conjunction with other mental health treatments, such as therapy or medication. However, incorporating healthy habits into daily life can improve overall mental health and well-being.

CHAPTER EIGHT
Exploring the Benefits of Mindfulness and Meditation

Mindfulness and meditation are practices that involve focusing on the present moment and accepting it without judgment. These practices have been shown to reduce stress, improve mood, and increase overall well-being. It can involve activities such as mindful breathing, mindful walking, or mindful eating. The goal is to focus on the present moment and accept it without judgment. This can help to reduce stress and improve overall well-being.

Meditation involves focusing the mind on a particular object, thought, or activity. This can include practices such as guided meditation, mantra meditation, or mindfulness meditation. Meditation has been shown to improve mood, reduce symptoms of anxiety and depression, and improve overall well-being. These are practices that require time and effort in order to be effective. However, incorporating these practices into daily life can improve overall mental health and well-being.

There are various ways to incorporate mindfulness and meditation into daily life. One effective way is to set aside a specific time each day for the practice, whether it's in the morning before starting the day, during a lunch break, or in the evening before bed. This can help establish a routine and make the practice a habit. Another way to incorporate mindfulness and meditation is to integrate it into daily activities. For example, while brushing teeth, focus on the sensation of the toothbrush against the teeth and the taste of toothpaste, rather than letting the mind wander. Similarly, while washing dishes, pay attention to the sensation of the water on the hands and the sounds of the dishes clinking together.

You can also practice mindfulness and meditation while engaging in other activities, such as yoga or tai chi. These practices combine physical movement with mindfulness, helping to reduce stress and promote relaxation. In addition to reducing stress and improving well-being, mindfulness and meditation have also been shown to have physical health benefits. Research has found that these practices can help to lower blood pressure, improve sleep, and reduce chronic pain. Practicing mindfulness and meditation are powerful tools that can improve mental and physical health.

CHAPTER NINE
Healing Trauma and Moving Forward

Trauma can have a lasting impact on mental health. However, there are many effective treatments available that can help individuals to heal and move forward. An effective treatment for trauma is trauma-focused therapy. This type of therapy involves working with a mental health professional to process the trauma and develop coping mechanisms. This can involve techniques such as exposure therapy or cognitive processing therapy. Group therapy and support groups can be helpful for individuals who have experienced trauma. These groups provide a safe and supportive environment for individuals to share their experiences and connect with others who have gone through similar experiences.

In addition to therapy, self-care activities can also be helpful in healing from trauma. This can involve activities such as exercise, healthy eating, and engaging in activities that bring joy. If you have experienced trauma, seek help from a mental health professional. Trauma is a serious condition that can impact all areas of life, but with proper treatment, it is possible to heal and move forward.

Healing from trauma is a process that takes time and may involve setbacks. However, with the support of a mental health professional and the implementation of self-care practices, individuals can learn to manage their symptoms and move forward towards healing and recovery.

CHAPTER TEN

Effective Communication Strategies for Mental Health

Effective communication is key to maintaining good mental health. It involves expressing emotions, thoughts, and feelings in a clear and constructive way. Good communication can help individuals to build stronger relationships, manage stress, and reduce symptoms of anxiety and depression.

An effective communication strategy is active listening. This involves listening to what the other person is saying and responding in a way that shows that you understand and care. It's important to avoid interrupting or dismissing the other person's feelings or thoughts. Another effective communication strategy is using "I" statements instead of "you" statements. For example, instead of saying "You always make me feel like this," try saying "I feel this way when this happens." This can help to avoid blaming the other person and instead focus on how you are feeling.

Practicing assertive communication is vital. It involves expressing your needs and boundaries in a clear and respectful way. It's important to avoid being passive or aggressive and instead aim for a balanced approach. By practicing effective communication, individuals can improve their mental health and build stronger relationships with others.

One other important strategy is to avoid making assumptions. It's important to clarify information and ask questions if necessary, rather than assuming you know what someone else is thinking or feeling. This can help to avoid misunderstandings and reduce stress. Another strategy is to express gratitude and appreciation. By expressing gratitude for the people and things in your life, you can improve your overall mood and strengthen relationships. This can involve simple actions such as saying thank you or writing a note of appreciation.

It's also vital to be mindful of nonverbal communication. Nonverbal cues such as body language, tone of voice, and facial expressions can have a significant impact on communication. Being aware of your own nonverbal cues and paying attention to others' cues can help to improve communication and reduce misunderstandings. Also, recognize when communication is not effective and take steps to address the issue. This can involve seeking help from a mental health professional, taking a communication skills course, or practicing active listening and other communication strategies.

CHAPTER ELEVEN
Navigating the Stigma Surrounding Mental Health

Stigma surrounding mental health can prevent individuals from seeking help and getting the treatment they need. It's important to understand the common misconceptions surrounding mental health and work to reduce the stigma. One common misconception is that mental health issues are a sign of weakness or a personal failing. However, mental health issues are a medical condition that can affect anyone, regardless of their strength or character.

Another common misconception is that individuals with mental health issues are dangerous or unpredictable. However, this is simply not true. In fact, individuals with mental health issues are more likely to be the victims of violence than the perpetrators. Hence, it's beneficial to educate oneself and others about mental health and work to reduce the stigma. This can involve talking openly about mental health, supporting mental health advocacy groups, and seeking out mental health resources when needed.

Reducing stigma around mental health can also involve advocating for policies and laws that prioritize mental health resources and support. This can include supporting mental health funding and research, as well as advocating for policies that increase access to mental health care. Additionally, it's crucial to challenge negative stereotypes and language surrounding mental health. This can involve speaking up when someone uses stigmatizing language or stereotypes, and using language that promotes understanding and empathy.

Sharing personal experiences about mental health challenges can help to reduce feelings of isolation and shame, and demonstrate that mental health issues are common and treatable. Also, prioritize self-care and seek help when needed. This can help to reduce the impact of stigma on one's own mental health, and demonstrate that seeking help is a normal and healthy choice.

CHAPTER TWELVE

Tools and Techniques for Maintaining Mental Wellness

Maintaining good mental health involves a variety of tools and techniques. This can include self-care activities such as exercise, healthy eating, and engaging in activities that bring joy. It can also involve seeking support from friends, family members, or a mental health professional.

Practicing stress management techniques such as meditation, deep breathing, or progressive muscle relaxation can help to reduce symptoms of anxiety and depression. It's important to find techniques that work for the individual and incorporate them into daily life.

Practicing gratitude is another activity for maintaining good mental health. It involves focusing on the things that you are grateful for in your life and acknowledging them. This can help to shift your mindset towards positivity and increase feelings of happiness and well-being.

Setting boundaries and prioritizing self-care can also help to maintain good mental health. This can involve saying "no" to activities that are not enjoyable or prioritize self-care activities such as exercise or spending time with loved ones.

Engaging in creative activities such as painting, writing, or playing music can also be beneficial for mental wellness. These activities can help to reduce stress, improve mood, and provide a sense of accomplishment and satisfaction.

Journaling is also a helpful tool for maintaining mental wellness. Writing down thoughts and feelings can help to process emotions and identify patterns or triggers that may be affecting mental health. It can also serve as a tool for reflection and self-discovery.

Finally, seeking social support and connecting with others is a crucial tool for maintaining good mental health. This can involve joining social groups, volunteering, or simply spending time with loved ones. Having a strong support network can provide a sense of belonging and help to alleviate feelings of loneliness or isolation. By incorporating these activities into your daily life, you can maintain good mental health and thrive in all areas of life.

CONCLUSION

Mental health is an essential aspect of our lives, and it's time to prioritize it. We hope this book has been a valuable resource for you on your mental health journey. We've covered a lot of ground, from understanding mental health to exploring coping mechanisms for managing stress and anxiety.

We've also delved into more challenging topics, like overcoming depression and negative thoughts and healing from trauma. Throughout the book, we've emphasized the importance of building resilience and maintaining mental wellness long-term.

We understand that navigating the stigma surrounding mental health can be challenging, but we hope this book has given you the tools and techniques to do so. Communication is a vital aspect of mental health, and we've provided strategies for effective communication.

We've also discussed the role of nutrition, exercise, mindfulness, and meditation in mental health, and we hope you've gained a better understanding of how these factors impact your mental wellness and how to incorporate them into your daily life.

Remember, mental health is not a one-time fix but a continuous journey. We encourage you to continue prioritizing your mental wellness and using the tools and techniques provided in this book. Your mind is a powerful tool, and unlocking its potential can have a significant impact on your life.

Thank you for reading this book, and we wish you all the best on your mental health journey.